The Positive Side of the Bad Stuff

LESLIE POGUE

The Positive Side of the Bad Stuff

Compilations of blogs
2nd Edition

Table of Contents

Introduction 4
Kiss From a Rose 4
Discovering Self As You Grow 8
Natural Mind 11
We're Off to See the Wizard 14
The Serenity of Traffic 16
Dazed and Confused 18
Go Do It Now! 20
L.I.F.E. – Look Inside For Everything 21
The Frienemy that Came to Dinner 23
Banish Your Demons on All Hollow's Eve 26

Our Need to Feel Safe 28
Get Uncomfortable 33
Fall into L.I.F.E. – Part I of IV 35
Fall into L.I.F.E. – Part II of IV 38
Fall into L.I.F.E. – Part III of IV 43
Fall into L.I.F.E. – Part IV or IV 45
New Beginnings 48
Know that You Deserve Your Dreams 49
5 Ground Rules for your Relationship to be All It Can Be 51
Random Acts of Kindness Week.......................53
Failure to Hit the Bullseye is Never the Fault of the Target! 56
State of Being 57
The Ego of Entitlement......................................59
Ruin is the Gift of Transformation 62
A New Hope 63
Humility 65
H.A.P.P.Y. 67
Why Doesn't God Use Neon? 69
Prayer...70

Positive Energy 73
Abundance 74
YES! 76
Are the Blues Dancin' on your Happy? 77
Are you living a WORK week or a LIFE week?. 78
There's a Reason Pampers are So Thick 82
Sometimes to Grow Up, You Gotta Meltdown! . 84
Dream Big! 88
If Life Were Santa's Lap, I'd Be the One Crying 92
Confront Your Fate 94
Back to the Middle 96
A Spring Song 98
Be Legendary 101
Going Deep 103
Control or Service? 105
The Silent Champion 107
Acceptance 108
You're not Scarlet O'Hara – You Just a Little Black Girl 109
I Am! 112

Introduction

The Positive Side of the Bad Stuff is a collection of blogs I've written over the last few years. It speaks primarily to the personal behaviors that we all manage every day from joy to grief to who cares to self-care.

It will give you a guide to make sense of the things in your life and find your positive side of the bad stuff.

Kiss From a Rose

August 31, 2010

This weekend I was honored to attend a memorial for my mentor's mother. It was very different because it wasn't in a church or even very formal. She has a beautiful garden in her backyard where she dug a hole, gave each person a long-stemmed rose and asked, those who wished to do so, to say something about her mother or a loved one they'd like to honor and put the rose in the hole so she could pour her mother's ashes over a bed of roses. She honored each person at the table for what they mean to her and/or what they meant to her mother. Her words weren't all flowery or prepared. She wasn't ever insulting but she spoke honestly from her heart about her friends and her mother. She called her brother who was in another state to join in on the part specific to their mother. And, she did all this over a family style meal that she and her son prepared including some of her mother's recipes while walking around in her mother's shoes. I found that especially touching.

Not coming from a family that freely expresses love or honest feelings; I was overwhelmed by all the love and respect that surrounded her. So, I found it odd that in speaking to one of her guests, she shared that the hostess, in planning this event, made the comment that she didn't have very many friends. The turn-out showed all evidence to the contrary but it made me think about what we think about our own lives and how oblivious most of us are to how we affect other people who come in and out of our lives.

As we get older, we face the inevitable circle of life, and if you haven't dealt with it prematurely, you will have to say goodbye to parents, uncles, aunts, grandparents, and maybe even some older siblings. What would you say about them? What would they say about you? I bet it's not what you think.

There is no way to know how many lives you impact or in what way your presence is felt. We touch lives in the grocery store, at the gas station, and even just crossing the street. A smile could make the difference in the life of a stranger. No words necessary.

There is a great goal setting exercise in eulogizing yourself. It helps you think about the things you want to accomplish in this life. The other is a bucket list. You can do that if you wish but today, I don't want you to write about a life that you plan to have. You know how you want to be remembered! Take action today! Call and volunteer to feed the homeless, sign up for a walk or a run, call a relative you haven't spoken to in who knows how long, just to say hi. Make it a habit.

I kept my rose because I've always wanted that kind of display with my friends and family but have mostly only seen it in movies. My rose is a reminder that it is real. I can have that too; I just have to make it happen. Today, in addition to investing in your financial future, invest in your emotional future by nurturing those closest to you.

Discovering Self as You Grow

August 23, 2010

As you grow in the knowledge and comfort of self, you may notice that you may not enjoy the same things; especially if some of the things that change are bad habits. I quit smoking about 7 years ago and along with that change I noticed that I don't like to drink as much. I also noticed, while in Vegas, that I now don't like to gamble as much either. They just seemed to go together, the cigarette in one hand as you hold your cards and the drink there by your side. Also, I've gone back to wine. Hard drinks like my cosmos and my white Russian just do not satisfy as they once did.

For whatever reason, recently, I was thinking about a trip I took to Hawaii once. I always imagined Hawaii as this island paradise with white sandy beaches, tropical rain, big waves, and an island feel. I stayed in downtown Honolulu which was smack dab in the city. I felt more like I was in New York instead of on an island paradise. It was noisy, smelly, crowded, full of traffic, and on the corner was a McDonalds, Starbucks, and a Subway. On the other corner was Red Lobster and Outback. Traveling alone I appreciated my familiar favorites but there was nothing pushing me out of my comfort zone. Don't get me wrong, my city view was beautiful, and the ocean was so blue but because I was in the city, I feel that I missed out on the true island experience. I learned that I should have rented a car or done a little more research and found a hotel on another part of the island. I did see the Pearl Harbor Memorial but again, I enjoyed the 20-minute movie they showed us before we went over to the actual memorial.

I said all that to say this.... I got caught up in the hype of "Hawaii" instead of spending a little extra time on planning how to do Hawaii for the things I like.

Not everyone likes to go parasailing and scuba diving. Not everyone has the budget to shop at the high-end stores like Prada and Tiffany that line the main strip. Some people go on vacation to see things and order room service, or just hang out while other people take care of you. I learned that for where I am in my life and especially if I am traveling solo, I need to make sure that I have the conveniences that make it a memorable experience for me and not try to fit into the cookie cutter idea of what I "should" want to do.

So, how much are you still adjusting to please others? Now don't confuse adjusting with compromise. There is nothing wrong with compromise. We must give up a little to co-exist with others effectively, but we do not have to give up ourselves. I really enjoy my grey hair but a friend of mine recently told me that it makes me look older than I am. I disagree; however, even if she is right, should I change me or should the people coming into my life take me as I am?

While money and men are two areas I am still learning to master, I refuse to change the person I am at my core, but I am more than willing to bend a little to allow another person in and sacrifice some luxuries to allow for financial growth.

Today, think about your life and if you are being your true self. I admit that I have gotten off track myself and thinking about my

Hawaiian getaway was a friendly reminder that I'm Leslie, not my friends, not my mother. I'm me and I'm not the same materialistic person I used to be. For me simplicity is key, and I am willing to pay a little more for service and convenience, but the "STUFF" of life is not why I get up every morning.

Don't let things that seem like a great opportunity cloud your overall objective. It may seem like a good idea at the time but look deeper; perhaps a delay may actually move you further, faster. As you discover yourself you will realize so many changes along the way, especially as you age. Embrace the knowledge and use it to move forward.

Natural Mind

August 16, 2010

This week, I'm posting a story I read in "The Joy of Living – Unlocking the Secret & Science of Happiness", by Yongey Mingyur Rinpoche. I read this book some time ago, but this story always stays with me, and I wanted to share it with you.

It is an old story told by Buddha, about a very poor man who lived in a rickety old shack. Though he didn't know it, hundreds of gems were embedded in the walls and floor of his shack. Though he owned all those jewels, because he didn't understand their value, he lived as a pauper – suffering from hunger and thirst, the bitter cold of winter and the terrible heat of summer.

One day a friend of his asked him, "Why are you living like such a pauper? You're not poor. You're a very rich man."

"Are you crazy?" the man replied. "How can you say such a thing?"

"Look around you," his friend said. "Your whole house is filled with jewels – emeralds, diamonds, sapphires, rubies."

At first the man didn't believe what his friend was saying. But after a while he grew curious and took a small jewel from his walls into town to sell. Unbelievably, the merchant to whom he brought it paid him a very handsome price, and with the money in hand, the man returned to town and bought a new house, taking with him all the jewels he could find. He bought himself new clothes, filled his kitchen with food, engaged servants, and began to live a very comfortable life.

For so many years he didn't recognize what he possessed. It wasn't until he recognized what he already had that he freed himself from poverty and pain.

It's the same for all of us. As long as we don't recognize our real nature, we suffer. Whether we recognize it or not, though, its qualities remain unchanged. But when you begin to recognize it in yourself, you change, and the quality of your life changes as well. Things you never dreamed possible begin to happen.

Today I challenge you to recognize the gems within you and their worth. Take them into the world expecting to be paid handsomely for who you are; in the currency of good friends, healthy relationships, the joy of giving, a career you can't wait to get to everyday and of course…. money. You CAN live the comfortable life you deserve.

We're Off to See the Wizard

August 9, 2010

One of my favorite movies is the Wizard of Oz. It occurred to me while facing a very challenging task this week that sometimes we come up against the Wizard. The scene that popped in my mind was when Dorothy and crew go to the wizard to ask for help for Dorothy to get back home. He yells and belittles our heroes and finally gives them a task, "Bring me the broomstick of the wicked witch of the west and I will grant your requests. Now Go! I SAID GO!"

We are living in a gut check time in our history and while some have made the misdiagnosis that it has never happened before, you must recognize that this is not new but, the primary difference is that instead of our parents shouldering the burden, now it's us in the hot seat of responsibility.

There are times in our lives when we must be completely naked before the world. Our most vulnerable position is uncovered and is at the mercy of decision makers. In those moments, even the most unshakeable soul can feel intimidated, defeated, and exposed as a fraud.

Living and being in the world brings crossroads. These crossroads can go by the name of divorce, death, eviction, bankruptcy, and unemployment. In those life moments, you inevitably must face the Wizard. Go into those moments prepared. Do everything you can do even if that is all you did the whole day or week. Stand your ground and don't give up. Even though Dorothy was scared, she still faced the wizard, trembling knees, and all. And…she took some friends with her for support. My experience in those moments have been of people in position, pontificating and puffing out their ego in an effort to make you feel smaller which is actually a sign of their own insecurity.

When standing before the wizard, always remember and don't ever forget that in spite of all that smoke and fire, when you pull back the curtain to see what's really going on….
he's just a man!

The Serenity of Traffic

August 3, 2010

How would you like to have your very own special place where you can listen to the kind of music you like or none at all; where there is no, "I want", "I need", "can you get"; where you are in total control of the comfort level? That would be fantastic huh?

Well, you do.... TRAFFIC. It's easy to focus on the negatives of traffic; the exhaust fumes of the cars in front of you, the 3-5 mile an hour roll/stop that goes on for 45 minutes, and of course the extra hour you have to get up and leave in the morning to accommodate this break down in transportation engineering.

But what if you were able to use that time to your benefit? Think of it as your own private office where there are no interruptions. You can return calls (using a hands-free device of course), you can record thoughts and your plans or goals, you can talk to yourself without anyone thinking you're crazy. I mean seriously, have you seen the things people do in their car in traffic? Everything from reading the paper to shaving. It's a gosh darn hazard out there!

Basically, what I'm saying is, instead of trying to control the situation by getting angry and darting in and out of traffic, embrace it. You are at the mercy of everyone that got there before you did so use that time for you. That is probably the only time of the day when you are completely alone. How many opportunities do you get where you are actually allowed to be alone and think of no one but yourself? I'm guessing not too many. Well, in traffic you are the captain of your domain. Take control of your ship and give yourself the gift of peace. I like to play car games like pick two cars and have them race to a certain point while I do the commentary of who's inching ahead the fastest. One day I noticed that registration tags are two different colors depending on whether you registered in the first half of the year or the second. I know…. you're saying that I have way too much time on my hands but in traffic, you're right! I do, so why not be entertained?

While everyone around you is frowned up and tense, create your own nirvana and arrive at your destination, rejuvenated by self-care, belly laughs, and special you time because now you know *THE SECRET*....

TRAFFIC is your friend!

Dazed and Confused

September 27, 2010

These days, so many things are going on and you are moving so fast that it is easy to lose your balance. Between evictions, moving, bankruptcy, work, kids, new homes, old neighborhoods, we can easily feel confused.

In the midst of new environments, and lost loved ones, how do we maintain the happy? You have to allow yourself to feel what you're feeling. The world doesn't need to know that you may want to curse or cry but you can admit it to yourself. There is a difference between settling and giving into your situation and making peace with it.

If you are settling, you have essentially given up. Exercising is out the window, the bad food is back, and so much for a schedule. TV has become your best friend. How's that workin' for ya? Settling isn't gonna get it done. You must make peace with what is happening now. It is ok! Life happens to the best of us. It's what you do in those situations that define who you are. Allowing yourself to veg out is a band-aid and does not attack the root issue. Exploration of your fear can clue you into the root cause.

Finding peace is a much healthier approach. Right where you are now, pause, take a deep breath in, exhale, and again. Now one last time with your eyes closed. Just changing your breathing can soothe your body into a more relaxed state. Now, look around at where you are. Repeat after me…" This is temporary! This is temporary! This is temporary! This is temporary!" The key to finding peace is understanding that you don't have to like the situation, but you must move past it. Take action. Develop a plan complete with rewards and penalties. Be honest about what you are capable of today. If you can't party today, don't; but don't allow yourself to hibernate either.

Being dazed and confused is normal during major transition. Be aware of your breathing, look at your current situation as a beginning instead of an ending, and make a plan toward the next phase of your life and you will begin to see clearly.

Go Do It Now!

September 20, 2010

This week I'm gonna **KISS** you all. I'm gonna **K**eep **I**t **S**imple **S**weetie!

This weekend I was reminded of the lifestyle that I deserve, that I enjoy, that I am going after with gusto!

This week all I'm saying to you is...GO FOR IT!

Go visit the life you want via an event. Go sit next to the type of guy or girl you want in a social situation. Go walk in the halls of the building you want to work in. When you can actually see yourself doing it, your brain will catch up and believe you and you will live it.

This week, this phrase is NOT allowed: I can't afford it. I'm not saying go spend your life savings, I'm just saying STOP SAYING THAT!

You can do whatever you want. GO DO IT! NOW!

L.I.F.E. – Look Inside for Everything

September 14, 2010

This week I've been surrounded by transition. A move to a new city, a test that can change your career, empty nest, or just the prospect of getting a new job; people in my life as well as myself have either had a major life transition or is embarking on a major life change.

When change happens, and it always will, we tend not to see it as a good thing. The thing about change and transition is that it's movement. Even if you feel like you've taken a step back, chances are that you are moving forward on the current phase of your journey, and you're probably still stuck on what you think "should" be happening. Movement is good!

Now pause for a moment and give yourself a chance to wrap your head around what is or is about to happen.

This is the time to look within. A pause is allowed. Stop and think about how you want the next phase to play out. What's working, what isn't, what you can't control and what you already have control of. Here's a hint...it's not nothing! There are things that you already control. I double dog dare you to write down at least five. Go ahead, you know you can't resist a dare.

Remember, LIFE happens but at those moments, you already have the tools to be A-Mazing. Look Inside For Everything! Listen to your heart, your spirit, the nervous tummy, and the headaches. All of these are clues about what you already want. Pay attention, your gas is telling you something.

Take the time to say NO for one day. Take a little longer in the shower in the morning. Self-care is critical during transition. Life is great about reminding you of all the things you *need* to do except taking care of you unless you pay attention.

Look Inside For Everything – Enjoy LIFE!

The Frenemy that Came to Dinner

September 6, 2010

We all have that favorite shirt or skirt are dress or whatever it is in our closet that no longer fits; either because it no longer fits physically or is not age appropriate. Whatever it is we hold on to it because we love that dress or that top or that skirt because they conjure up memories of, I don't know, better days, better times, or maybe our youth. Even if it's a goal to get back in that outfit, the bottom line is it's dated, and it no longer fits. It doesn't fit the current you.

As you move along in your growth, you get to a place where some of the people in your life, the places in your life, the things that you're holding on to, no longer fit because you move into another level of wisdom, of knowledge, and of peace and when that happens you have to recognize what stuff to throw away or push to the side.

I had the opportunity to go out with an old friend of mine. The memories we share are immeasurable. There are no words for the time we spent together back in the day. Our lives today are very different, or should I say, my life today is very different, and her life is still very much the same in a lot of ways. My eyes were opened, possibly for the first time, because when we were dining, once again, she felt the need to go back down memory lane, to my detriment. While memory lane is a nice place to visit, it is not a place that I like to conjure up with any regularity.

The thing about my 20's is that I had a great time because I was young and I did what I wanted; in my 30's I was reckless and bitter and angry; so now in my 40's, all that is behind me, where it belongs.

Just listening to her talk, reminded me of a conversation I had with my mother about self-worth. What I found interesting is throughout the entire conversation, even though I'm very proud of my accomplishments, especially right now, it never occurred to me to change the topic of conversation to a more positive representation of my life. It didn't even hit me until a couple of days later. I couldn't curtail what she was saying to get the conversation off of my wild and crazy days in my 20's to the book I've written, the blog I write, the career that I have today, my entertainment accomplishments, the charities I support, not even the beautiful man that was sitting next to me. I was caught so off guard that my old self-doubting habits crept in, and I took it.

Needless to say, on the one hand I recognize that there are some things better left in my past, I also have to extract the fact that there are some people that we move beyond as well. I really didn't deserve to be the focal point of that conversation. My efforts to honor a friend that doesn't honor me reminded me of that favorite t-shirt I held on to for years. It was hard but ultimately, I gave it away.

So, the lesson here is to definitely look at your life and declare, HERE'S WHAT I DESERVE; HERE'S MY WORTH and that includes the way people talk to you and about you. You have to value yourself. If you don't then you could find yourself in the belly of a volcano that you mistakenly thought was dormant.

You are better than that!

Banish Your Demons on All Hollow's Eve

October 25, 2010

This week we embark on All Hollow's Eve, a.k.a., Halloween. Instead of dwelling on the scary stuff, perhaps, it is a good time to focus on All Saints. Celts believed this was a very important day to celebrate, as this was the day when two worlds, the living and the dead, came together. So, let this week be in honor of your past and your present.

Some of us have a very scary past but, it is our past that has made us who we are today. The loves we've had and lost, the jobs that drove us nuts and that pushed our limits while giving us skills that we may not have known we gained, the family members that we miss and cherish even in their absence, and the life choices that sent us on journeys that we never expected but have now blossomed from.

All Hollow's Eve is the precursor for All Saint's Day when it is believed that all past spirits come back to haunt the living. Don't let your past continue to haunt you. Whatever is resting there should be buried now and if you haven't completely put it behind you, now is a great time. Make a list of all the things that are still haunting your thoughts. That's right...ALL OF THEM! Be honest with yourself. Once you have your list, find a safe place to *set it on fire* and as it goes up in smoke, I want you to say repeatedly, I release you, there is only room for abundance here; I release you, there is only room for abundance here; I release you, there is only room for abundance here. And with that...let it go!

As we go into the last two months of this year, don't wait until the New Year to start cleaning house. Start exercising and eating right now, start managing your money now, and take care of yourself now.

Life doesn't have to be scary so exorcise those demons that may haunt your thoughts. They are no match for the strength and determination that gives you the courage to face each day and conquer all that life likes to "Trick or Treat" us with. (sorry...you knew it was coming)

You are AWESOME! Have a Great Week!

Our Need to Feel Safe

October 19, 2010

In our current environment, safety is a huge issue. We discuss our safety almost daily, post 911, but are we any safer than before 911? I think we are more aware of our vulnerability, but I don't know that I am convinced we are any safer. According to the TSA we are at Yellow – Elevated status. The Five levels from lowest to highest threat is Green – Low, Blue – Guarded, Yellow – Elevated, Orange – High, and Red – Severe. Since its inception in 2001, I do not recall ever making it to Guarded or Low. The TSA site also shows a grid that represents 20 Layers of

Security.(http://www.tsa.gov/press/speeches/111507_hawley_house.shtm) which is described in an eight page testimony by Kip Hawley, Assistant Secretary but again I ask, are we safer? If you feel that you are, then you are.

It has been proven that we can be caught off guard, so theoretically, it can happen again. However, like getting hit by a car, if we thought about what "could" happen we'd never leave home. The fact is that if we thought about all the things that are going on in the world, we may feel too depressed, anxious, stressed, or dare I say it...scared to stay functional. Our hormones play a large part in managing our "fight or flight" response. When a person is emotionally stimulated, the adrenal glands release the hormones epinephrine (adrenalin) and norepinephrine (noradrenalin) into the bloodstream. Long known to be involved in the "fight or flight response," these hormones enable us to survive, and they also imprint powerful and enduring memories of the circumstances surrounding threatening situations. By controlling the input of frightening situations or even knowledge like news or scary movies, we suppress this fight or flight response and keep it manageable to maintain a "comfortable" lifestyle.

Isn't it nice when you come home? Don't you feel like you have left the rest of the world behind as if you have suddenly gone into your very own protective bunker? Coming home brings with it a sense of security just by virtue of being home and done with your interaction with the world. What if home does not feel safe due to abuse or your surroundings? This environment can also produce the fight or flight response. So how do we protect ourselves? How do we feel safe?

I have mentioned things that were within our control in earlier conversations. We have no control over the outside world but how we react to it is completely within our control. As long as you know you are doing what you can to improve the situation, then that is all you can do. I recently had a conversation about conservation and while I don't do a lot, I am aware enough to ration my water when I water my lawn and not use my hose to wash my car. I only run a full load of dishes and laundry and for just one person, you know I have got to stock up on underwear or I would be in some serious trouble. I recycle my grocery bags as trash bags, and I do not go to the Big Dog gas stations to passively boycott the inflated gas prices. I run in the Revlon Run/Walk and the AIDs Walk every year and I give periodically to Goodwill and similar organizations to help others. Knowing that I am doing what I can, I only watch the morning news and I read news articles online, but I do not pay attention to the security levels and all the political mudslinging about the things in the world and all the things they "promise" they will fix when they get in office. I am obviously informed; I just choose to be in control of what information comes into my world/home to affect my level of safety. You must do the same. Of course we can all probably do more but why focus on what we "could" be doing. Let's give ourselves credit for what we do, within our own individual ability to manage our own illusion of safety. Remember: "The wise man in the storm prays to God, not for safety from danger, but deliverance from fear." Ralph Waldo Emerson

Some suggestions:

1. Limit the amount of violent news stories and "drama" television that you watch daily
2. Discuss and implement a safety plan with your family in case of fire, earthquake, or intruder.
3. Manage the things your family watches and is exposed to on the internet and on television. There are Parental Guides for a reason and some children should not be exposed to certain shows or movies.
4. TALK to the members of your family, especially if you have children. Open discussions invite trust and safety. If your family members feel they can talk to you without being attacked (that includes our spouses) then they are more likely to share. Encourage communication.
5. Be aware. Make eye contact and be confident.
6. Listen to your gut. If you feel in danger, do what you need to do to get to a safe place immediately.
7. Visit http://www.sacsconsulting.com/safetytips.htm for additional tips on safety

REMEMBER - The door to safety swings on the hinges of common sense. ~Author Unknown

Reference: S. Wood, E. Wood, and D. Boyd (2005) The World of Psychology (5th ed.), Pearson Education Inc.

Get Uncomfortable

October 5, 2010

Have you ever jumped out of a plane? Have you ever MC'd a concert? Have you ever moved to a place where you don't know the customs? All of these can easily make you uncomfortable. Stepping outside of what you know takes, courage, faith, and a plan is highly recommended but not always available.

When you dare to do something, you've never done before, no matter how big or small, you are being vulnerable to the universe. You are saying, I'm open to the possibility; the "what if".

Our day-to-day responsibilities make it easy for us to cop-out of pushing the envelope. "It's late," "I'm tired", "maybe next weekend", are common reasons (more like excuses) for not trying something new.

Remember how fun it was to discover that you had a talent for something or just that you learned something new? Our lives need that. Shake things up a bit. Take a dance class instead of going to the gym today, glaze a pot with your daughter, or take a ride on your husband's motorcycle with him.

Get uncomfortable a little. Because the moment you stop growing and learning, is the moment you shut down and disappear.

The world needs you too much for you to let that happen. So, go on…get uncomfortable. It's fun!

Fall into L.I.F.E. – Part I of IV

November 2, 2010

Now that we're into Fall, it's time to really begin to go inside and look at where you are and where you want to go. Today is the Midterm election and we are making choices on our political future. Today, take a step toward your emotional and physical future. For the five weeks of November, I will be giving you tools to **L**ook **I**nside **F**or **E**verything (L.I.F.E.). This week's topic:

Commit to Commitment

To commit is to decide. To choose to stick with a decision no matter what happens. When we commit to doing something that others don't understand, we are often met with opposition when unless the decision is against the law or harmful to yourself or others, what you need most at that moment is support. But how do we know when they're right or when we are making the right decision for ourselves? Notice I didn't leave it at "right decision" because there is no such thing. What is right for one is not always right for all so it comes back to knowing yourself; that is how you will know if you are going along with someone else's will or following your own passion. There will be plenty of people in your life that will tell you that whatever decisions you are about to embark upon are wrong. It is up to you to follow through or give in to the masses.

Your ability to be assertive and know yourself allows you to set boundaries. Committing to a decision is not trusting in others or an outside source; committing to a decision is to trust yourself; trusting that you have done your homework and are equipped to be a good critical thinker. Heuristics or general rules of thumb help guide our critical thinking which allows us to commit to commitment.

Commitment also requires humility, desire, and dedication. Just like the stock market, which has never lost money over a 20-year period, the decisions we make can be volatile, but they can also be lucrative and stimulate growth as well as seem effortless over time and consistent behavior.

Never be afraid to say no! By setting goals and standing firm in your own personal objectives you will know when an opportunity is a dividend or a detour. So how do you rally when your commitment takes a detour? You re-evaluate! Use critical thinking and keep what is working and readjust what isn't. Donald Trump and Walt Disney had many do-overs on their journey to success, but they never gave up or said it can't happen. As a result, their success is legendary.

Nothing will come of doing nothing. So, in order to progress, you must make the decision about what kind of life you want. I woke up one day and wanted to know what happy feels like. Going on that journey required me to work for it. I asked the hard questions of family and friends, lost some people along the way, and cried a lot! But the peace I feel on the other side of that mountain is amazing. There is always work to do to maintain my happiness and I fall into old habits sometimes, but I now see the signs and can rally quickly and regain control of the life I want to live. Committing to a happy, fulfilled life is very broad with a number of tasks required along the way for you to obtain and sustain it, like being assertive, setting boundaries, and living a value-added life including only allowing value added people to be center stage with you. Remember – You deserve the best! Settling is not an option – EVER!

Today – Commit to the commitment of living an amazing life!

Quote of the Week – "Commitment unlocks the doors of imagination, allows vision, and gives us the "right stuff" to turn our dreams into reality." James Womack

Fall into L.I.F.E. – Part II of IV

November 9, 2010

This week's topic: **Visual Reality**

Visualization is a significant tool that gives you the power to realize your goals by first seeing yourself in your mind. The premise of "The Secret" discusses the law of attraction and how visualization by first manifesting in the mind can then go to work to bring your deepest ambitions to you.

Now, don't misunderstand, visualization alone will not magically make your dreams come true, it's not voodoo. However, visualization can give you your own reality show playing in your head. You still have to do the work.

Visualization can be intangible, in the mind, and tangible via photos or a poster. Visualization through meditation takes discipline but cannot only help you see yourself achieving your dreams, but it is very relaxing and relieves stress. Visualization through meditation or affirmation is best done in the evening before bed because you are relaxed, and your thoughts go into your subconscious and work on your behalf. Using affirmations is another way to visualize your goals. By writing out a script in the affirmative of how you want things to be, i.e., I have $50,000.00 in savings, I am running my own *fill in the blank* company, etc., and saying it out loud daily, you are speaking your life into being. Remember, "If you can imagine it, you can achieve it; if you can dream it, you can become it." You know – See It! Believe It! Achieve It!

Well known sleep researcher J. Allen Hobson's theory is that when we dream, it is our mind's way of working through the things that are happening in our lives. By planting the seed of how we want our life to look, we utilize the brain activity that is already happening and the law of attraction to summon the things and people we need to move forward to come to us.

Tangible visualization can be as small as a card with your affirmation on it that you refer to everyday or you can make a poster. I call it a "Happy Chart." A happy chart has specific pictures of what you want to achieve. If there are people in your pictures, they should reflect you. If one of your goals is a car, it should be the specific car and color you want. Make it fun! Use magazines, pictures online, clipart, catalogues, and even scrapbooking accessories to make it more personal. The most important thing is to be specific.

Meditative Visualization – Today I am ready to live the life I deserve. I am focused and driven to be happy!

Complete your meditative visualization script. Begin with the two sentences above and write out your goals. If you want to lose weight, then state, I am _blank_ pounds. I own _fill in the blank_ restaurant where I have enjoyed profits since I opened. You get the pattern. If you need a little time, that's ok. Make a list of how you'd like to see your life. You may even want to close your eyes and try to visualize living one of your biggest goals. Don't get caught up in the "ifs". "If I didn't have kids," "If I had more money", "If I didn't work full-time" **FORGET THAT!** This is on the premise that all systems are on **GO!** Don't worry about those other things in your life; they will take care of themselves as you realize your dreams. First you must have the vision that you can.

You can also record your visualized affirmation and play it while you meditate on it. This may make it easier to get in the habit. But, keep in mind, the actual visual chart adds to your focus because it puts it on paper. It's something you can check off periodically and see your progress. You can always do that later if you wish but it is a valuable tool.

It is well worth it! And……SO ARE YOU!

Quote of the Week – To accomplish great things, we must not only act, but also dream; not only plan, but also believe." Anatole France, French writer (1844-1924)

Fall into L.I.F.E. – Part III of IV

November 22, 2010

This week's topic: **Listening to the little man inside.**

Double Indemnity is one of my favorite movies (one of many) and Edward G. Robinson's character is the manager at an Insurance Agency. When Fred McMurry's character submits a claim for a saucy customer, played by Barbara Stanwick, Edward's little man makes his appearance. He keeps saying throughout the movie, my little man is never wrong. AND NEITHER IS YOURS.

Our instincts guide us through the rocky river that is life. When we listen, we are usually met with calm seas but when we don't, we hit a pocket of deep water that hopefully doesn't take us under the current.

As we grow, we will be presented with tests that show us how much we've learned from past experiences. How we react in those moments can be overwhelming and inspiring if we recognize the growth.

I was recently put in an interesting situation. I was on a date and there came a point that seemed very odd and frankly, a little unsafe. In the past, I would have gone with it because of course, "I want him to like me." However, this time, I verbalized my discomfort and while I will never know for sure, I got a strong feeling that I dodged a potentially life changing bullet. Part of the reason I feel that way is that I got the full court press before this date and Casper after. I recognized the signs that had been sent to me with a vengeance the previous weeks and when I found myself, face to face with my lesson, I passed. I felt it immediately.

In life, we all have that little man (or woman) inside us that warn us that we are either repeating a previous misstep or we are about to. More often than not, we don't listen and later wonder…what the what? The life you live is your guide. Your experiences help you make better choices later even if you think that you haven't made good decisions up to this point. The consequence that resulted from that decision, still taught you something, if you were paying attention.

Don't wait for your New Year's Resolution; start making better choices today. Listen to that little voice inside. It knows you; it sees you; it loves you.

Fall into L.I.F.E. – Part IV or IV

November 22, 2010

This week's topic: **THANKSGIVING**

This week, we come together. Family flies in or out after getting felt up at the airport; mothers, aunts, and grandmothers everywhere are checking with Martha and the Neely's while planning the day, and eyes are rolling all across the nation at the thought of spending the day with OMG...Family!

As much as we love our families, this time of year can be very wearing on our mental health. This is a time, more than any other, for self-care. This is not license to emotionally eat or throw your hands up and wait until the holidays are over. Oh contraire. This is a time to really look within and find your own personal joy and strength and bring that to the family table.

How do you do that if you are facing your own challenges? Well, you can remember what you already know…this is temporary. And while it helps to compartmentalize through the tough stuff, what about those times that are precious? No matter how we feel about our families, these are memories that build the stories of our lives. You will never get these moments back. You have a starring role in how the day goes. You can be the hero or the villain; the headliner or the snarky best friend; the reason why most people typically hate getting together OR you can show them the joy, the strength, the appreciation or should I say…thanksgiving you have learned to have for this life.

Be present in this day. Talk to your family, be with them, hug them, laugh with them. Really listen to what is important to them. Make it a goal to learn one new thing about someone or a few someone's in your family. Let your life just be a blip on the day as you catch up with people who genuinely care and love you (whether you feel it or not).

Be thankful that you have people who love you. If you are away from family, call and catch up, send a card or an ecard to make your loved one's feel more special. Hold on to that one thing that you are thankful for, put it in your pocket or purse, and bring that with you to dinner. So, no matter how that day turns out, you will be beaming from inside. Happy Happy Joy Joy!

New Beginnings

January 14, 2011

They say that every day is another chance to do it right. We look to New Years as a time to start a diet, exercise routine, savings, etc. Gimmicks don't work. Why lie to yourself again? Instead, today, just promise you'll do your best. That's it, that's all. Not, I'll try to do my best; because, in the words of Yoda, "Try not; do or do not, there is no try." Just do your best every day and begin a lifestyle.

Eat well because it's the right thing to do, exercise any way you can because it's good for you and it's the right thing. Handle your business NOW because it's the right thing to do. Start saving and be kind to people why??…… say it with me……. because it's the right thing to do.

So, at this time of new beginnings…. for you and everyone around you…… just do your best and do the right thing!

Happy New Year!

Know that You Deserve Your Dreams

February 20, 2011

I was catching up on my TV shows and was watching Oprah's "Your OWN Show." This week's challenge was to do a Press Junket. In one of the interviews, when asked what you have learned, Zack, one of the contestants, said he learned that he deserves his dream. That was like a thunder bolt! I got chills. I had to speak on that.

What was so timely about it was that I had just had dinner with a friend of mine, and he was sharing the story of the way his parents love each other and that he wants that kind of love but doesn't know if he deserves it. That had the exact opposite effect, and it really broke my heart. He is one of the sweetest guys I know with such a big heart but for him to not feel that he deserves love, was sadly a familiar story.

Self-worth is different from self-esteem. You can know that you are the best thing since sliced bread, but do you know that you deserve the very best of everything? And you already possess it! We've been taught that it is selfish to think of self but what a lot of us didn't get was the disclaimer that it is just fine to think of self as long as you also think of others. Self-love may be something you need to practice. I had to practice it and I still practice it today. I am now very aware of my worth and live it every day but, sometimes I have moments when I forget that not only am I a wonderful being, but I deserve the joy and peace that I am finally aware, has always been there.

Say it with me now – *OUT LOUD*.... I DESERVE ALL THE GIFTS OF THE UNIVERSE. I DESERVE LOVE, ABUNDANCE, JOY, AND PEACE IN MY LIFE AND ALL THAT COMES WITH THAT!

Use that as your affirmation for this week. Whenever you are having a moment of doubt or worry or fear, just repeat that affirmation to yourself. Feel it as you say it. Make it more than just words because......*You're Worth It!*

5 Ground Rules for your Relationship to be All It Can Be

February 14, 2011

How do you have the relationship you always wanted? What can you do to either attract or improve your romantic relationships? Here are 5 simple things you can do.

1. First you must be the person you want in your life. If you are looking for someone who is kind and positive, successful, and secure, and healthy and fit; you must begin by being those things. It's never too late to become the person you want.
2. Truth and Honesty above all else – even if it will hurt a little. A healthy relationship should be a safe place to be honest. Remember the truth doesn't have versions so what you tell your mate should always be the absolute truth even if it's hard to hear. Learn how

to fight fair with each other and never go to bed angry.
3. Be an active participant in the relationship. Most of us say we want a 50/50 love but let's be real.... some days it's 60/40, some days it's 70/30, and unfortunately, some days it's as little as 80/20 but those ratios should rotate. When you put your mate's needs before your own (I don't mean never do anything for yourself) you take the focus off of yourself and if you are both doing it, then your needs are met anyway. You do have to let your mate know what your needs are, they aren't mind readers. Ask questions and share your needs along the way so you each know what you can do to make things that much better for your mate as their needs change because they do throughout the life of your relationship.
4. Allow someone to love you. That may sound silly, but you'd be surprised at how difficult it is for some people to let someone love them." Why didn't he....", "She never........", "I wish my spouse would........" Instead of focusing on the things they don't do, focus on the things

they do. And.... Are you doing those things? Recognize effort even when execution doesn't quite hit the mark.
5. Lastly.... don't make a bunch of rules. Love is organic not orchestrated. The book The Rules was supposed to be a poke at dating – I hope. At any rate, true love is natural, not forced, it simply is. Don't try to fit a square peg in a round hole. Just let it be. Hopefully the one you love will return your affection but if not, then there is someone better suited for you. They can't come into your life until the path is clear.

Don't force love, just let love.

Happy Valentine's Day!

Random Acts of Kindness Week

February 12, 2011

How far you go in life depends on you being tender with the young, compassionate with the aged, sympathetic with the striving and tolerant

of the weak and the strong. Because someday in life, you will have been all of these.
– George Washington Carver

So where are you in your journey? I'll bet, no matter where you are, you could stand to hear a kind word or just have someone do something nice for you. So, do unto others as you would have them do unto you.

This week is Random Acts of Kindness Week. What a great time to begin a new habit. Each day, choose to do something for someone else just because. You don't have to go out of your way; simply open a door for someone whose hands are full, call a relative you haven't spoken to in a while, or make a cake and take it to a neighbor. Ideally, we are sharing our kindness daily, but life does what life does, and we get caught up in our own stuff. At least for this week, put others first and notice not only how good you feel, but how much goodness comes your way as well.

Side effects of kindness may include but are not limited to…. sudden sense of feeling awesome, the attraction of others, a healthy glow coupled with really good mojo, as well as an uncontrollable urge to smile all the time. Be careful, it could be overwhelming at first but WOW! What a kick! Go on and getchu some!

Remember: Kindness, like a boomerang, always returns. –Author Unknown

Failure to Hit the Bullseye is Never the Fault of the Target!

February 7, 2011

Is your arrow sharp? Is your aim straight? When we go for our goals and we come up short, it's real easy to blame outside conditions. While there may be some outside factors, it is more often than not, our own skills that need to honed.

Every day is a new opportunity to do things better. Instead of getting frustrated with the progress or lack thereof, RE-EVALUATE and put together a new plan. It's never too late. Some of the most successful people in the world, became successful later in life.

CLARIFY your own strengths. Take a moment to right down all the things you do well, whether they are work related or not. Just do a brain dump of all the things you enjoy doing and that you do well. From that list, bump it up against the life you're living and see if you are doing any of them. Once you have a clear picture of what you do well, incorporate them into your life, read, study, learn, practice, and just be the best at it.

Once you have built up your confidence by learning and practicing your skills all you can, it is time to SHARE. Teach others, volunteer, help people around you. By giving back, your self-esteem and confidence grows and spills over into other areas of your life. You'll walk taller, smile bigger, and laugh more.

Remember – Our resources are abundant. There is enough for all of us. Go on and get yours!

State of Being

February 2, 2011

We are hearing about the State of the Union and the State of the State but what is your State? How is your current state of being?

As the new year is well on its way, it's a good idea to do an internal check in early to make sure you've started off on the right foot. Try not to focus so much on the big picture goals but just how you are right now. Are you enjoying getting up every day? Are you excited about your plans for your goals? Or.... are you back to being frustrated and not sure of what direction to go in?

When you evaluate early, you have time to take a step back. Follow these steps to ensure your state of being is balanced so you can proceed as needed, when needed:

1. **Act as if all your needs are met** - when you are not acting out of desperation or anxious about whatever, your head is clear to make better choices including additional preparation for backup alternatives.
2. **Center yourself at the beginning and the end of your day** – Spend five minutes sitting in silence or guided mediation in the morning and before you go to bed. In the morning, it will give you an opportunity to visualize how you'd like your day to go, and, in the evening, it helps give you restful sleep because you have taken the time to clear your mind of the day's minutiae.

3. **Do one thing fun each day (each week at the outside)** - Act like a kid. I carry a sack of jacks with me everywhere I go. I may never pull them out but when I need a kid moment, I'm ready. Go ride a bike, go skating, or just walk in the grass in your bare feet. Fit in one fun thing per day (week). That can also include one comfort food thing. Give yourself a treat for just getting up every day!

The Ego of Entitlement

April 24, 2011

Today is Easter Sunday. A day of resurrection. An opportunity to start today to be the person you want to be. At my place of worship, I volunteered to usher the last service. Now, historically, holiday Sundays are more frequented than regular Sunday's, but you add the fact that it is later in the day (11am) and you get the crowd of a lifetime – at least to me. I was not expecting what I saw.

Because of the crowd, we needed to ask people to wait to let them back in when they stepped out to the restroom or for whatever reason. While I can appreciate their feeling on the fact that they already had a seat, our requests were not personal. We were merely doing a job that involved keeping them safe as well as allowing those in the sanctuary an opportunity to have their worship without the interruption of people constantly moving around. There was even on instance where a celebrity; who shall remain nameless, but his actions were true to every character I've seen him play; sauntered up to my usher partner, with an intimidating, towering posture, only to finally be able to ask him if waiting would be a waste of his time. I was floored.

People were pushy and would bum rush the door when it would open for someone else, and this was supposed to be a place of peace and love. We had to raise our voices and repeatedly ask people to back up so that we could manage the doors. Why did we need to go there? Did they feel so entitled to just do what they wanted to do in spite of our polite direction and requests? To be fair, no one ever got irate or blatantly rude, but the insistence of their positions made our job a lot harder and frankly, in my opinion, was completely uncharacteristic of spiritual beings.

So, I said all that to say this, what gives us, as human beings, the right to insert ourselves when we are not being attacked? So many people say that the world would be a better place if more people exercised patience. Do they realize that to exercise patience, requires humility and the abandonment of ego? There were other celebrities as well as non-celebrities that also had to wait and I didn't hear a peep. We were even complimented by one lady, who shall also remain nameless, on how well we were "holding it down".

The next time you feel riled and want to assert yourself, pause for a moment and think about the situation. Try to put yourself in their place. How would you like to be treated if you were in their shoes? Are they being attacking or are they just trying to do their job? Help 'em out. Set aside your ego, when others wish to be rude. I'm not saying to let people push you around, however; when we let go of the need to be right, and heard and seen, we have grown into a person that is void of ego and rich with self-esteem and self-worth. It's always your choice.

Big Hug!

Ruin is the Gift of Transformation

April 19, 2011

It would be so great if everything worked the way that it should...or would it? How much beauty has been discovered at the site of ruins? The Parthenon, the Coliseum, Aztec and Egyptian Pyramids, all have the signs of age and still we spend thousands of dollars to gaze at their wonder and magnificence.

When we lose everything, it can feel like we have been decimated and defeated. However, if you are able to see past the rubble you will experience a gift few people get.... a clean slate. You have the rare opportunity to do it ALL differently. What usually happens unfortunately is that we repeat the same behavior, end up in the same storm, and ask, "why does this keep happening to me"?

Now that you know the pattern; next time you find yourself at a familiar crossroad, pause for a moment and notice what is happening. Bells, whistles, and sirens should be going off. This time you will see what is about to happen and you will be able to choose to do it differently. (Not better or worse – just different)

Armed with new information, you are equipped to choose a different path and thereby avoiding that pile of debris again. Hurray! Congratulations!

You have actively transformed your life. Feels good huh?

Big Hug!

A New Hope

April 13, 2011

We all have an amazing "force" within us. As our lives evolve, we have moments of doubt and fear. It is in those moments where your faith and trust are most tested.

It's like when Luke went into the cave and asked Yoda what's in there? Yoda responds, "only what you take with you". We carry our baggage with us even when our arms appear to be free.

It's time to lighten your load and practice knowing that you already possess the strength, love, joy, abundance, and everything else you will ever need. I frequently repeat to myself, "all my needs are met" and "everything is working for my greater good". When I am feeling nervous or afraid, I say, "I am safe, protected, and loved in all that I do". By saying these simple phrases, I bring myself back to center and knowing that the "I Am" is within me and I can do all that is needed.

Find what works for you, a poem, a scripture, or just a few sentences that you can believe in your heart. Repeat your positive ideas or phrases, a.k.a. affirmations regularly and really begin to feel the truth in them.

Humility

May 30, 2011

To be humble means to have a modest opinion or estimate of your own importance. It does not mean that you are unimportant, nor does it mean that you are subservient or passive. It simply means that you no longer need to shine a spotlight on yourself and yell, "NOTICE ME!"

There is a great level of peace that comes once you reach a place of humility. You know that you know. To get to this place takes practice and more than that, it takes self-worth. Do you know your worth? One of the best movies I've ever seen about self-worth is The Joy Luck Club.

Do you know your worth? Not in dollars but on a much bigger level. We are all spiritual beings in a human existence. Do you treat yourself as such? When you have a healthy self-worth level, you don't allow others to disrespect you. A friend of mine fired his agent because his tone was often unnecessarily mean and condescending. He was just a toxic person, so my friend decided to find representation elsewhere. Remember, there is always another way to get to the same result.

When you can let the other person have the last word; when you no longer let your possessions inflate your ego; when you appreciate all that you have, whatever that is, but continue to strive for greater everything, internal and external; you are humble.

Practice being humble. It may feel as though you are being passive at first but hang in there. Once you live in the "I know that I know", then you no longer have the need to prove or announce that you're right all the time because you already know you are.

- Humility is not judgmental; it is open to all possibilities.
- Humility does not have an ego; it appreciates all things.
- Humility does not fight the lesson; it grows stronger and moves further in learning the lesson.

H.A.P.P.Y.

May 30, 2011

I talk a lot about getting to your happy and I'd like to give everyone some stepping-stones over the next five posts to work on in your own life.

There are many keys to obtaining and maintaining your happy, but I've narrowed it down to these five; **H**umility, **A**bundance, **P**ositive Energy, **P**rayer/Meditation, and **Y**es. While this is a very limited list, these five tools are certainly some of the main pillars of life that will give you the happy that you seek. Of course, there are so many others, universal love, peace, self-awareness; the list goes on and on. I have focused on the elementary five and hopefully they will bring you joy and a nice place to begin or continue your daily practice of getting and keeping your happy.

I'd also like to hear from you. If there is a topic or area that you are working on in your journey, feel free to post a comment. I'd love to begin a dialogue and help in any way I can.

Why Doesn't God Use Neon?

May 4, 2011

Those of us who live by faith believe that if we listen and follow where our spirit is being led to go, we will follow our own rightful journey.

Unfortunately, that message isn't always as clear as we would like. Why doesn't God use Neon?!?

Living by faith and listening can be challenging, especially when you are in the muck of things. What we must understand is that it is in those moments when we need to listen most. What happens is we get caught up in survival mode and forget to just STOP! Only when we STOP can we hear what our next move must be.

Practice being still. Practice not rushing. Practice patience. One of the best ways I've found to practice patience is to deliberately stand in the longest line at the supermarket, target, or Wal-Mart. Do not read the magazines, do not make or answer a call. JUST STAND THERE. And when someone wants to pull you into their negativity about waiting, simply say…" how often are we allowed to do nothing?" Embrace the luxury of just being. Whatever it is you are rushing to will still be there.

Once you have learned to just be in those quiet moments, you will be more available and alert to hear the messages being sent to you via, TV, neighboring conversations, someone else's concerns, or just your own quiet voice.

Begin to listen and trust. Don't second guess the message. It's ok if you don't understand it when it comes but trust it. Remember…that is the "I Am" within you.

Prayer

June 13, 2011

I want to open by saying, when I say prayer, I mean both literally, as well as relatively like deep thought or meditation.

When we turn within, we are able to get in touch with the "I AM" within us. As we seek answers to the things we face in our lives, we need the answer to be clear and organic.

Lots of people go workout, go have a cocktail, or just try to busy themselves with "things" to keep their mind off of the thing they seek an answer to. Avoidance never gets you closer to solving a problem. It's like in relationships when your partner may say, "I just need some space, or time alone". That rarely ends well. How can you work on a challenge from a distance? You have to face it. By going within, and being quiet with whatever you are facing, the answer can be made clear in the quiet.

Now, an answer may not come to you at that moment, but what you've done is you've told the universe, "I'm ready to face the reality of this situation. Please guide my next steps". Then you can walk away and busy yourself with the gym or "things" until one day, in a stolen moment, maybe just walking to your car after work, BAM! The answer is revealed. Your whole body will tell you and then you'll know your next move.

Remember – L.I.F.E. – Look Inside For Everything.

If you are being present in it, it will reveal itself to you.
Just be ready for what you get!

Positive Energy

June 3, 2011

Where does positive energy come from? Where can we get it? Guess what? You already have it. It may not be as close to the surface as you'd like but it is already in you.

Here's a fast way to tap into it. Are you ready? Make sure you're comfortable, sit up straight, shoulders back, eyes forward and.... SMILE! That's right, a big cheesy one. Get silly with it, really ham it up. Now...how do you feel? A little giddy? Kinda light? Yep – that's powerful stuff. No preservatives added and it's completely free of charge. And best of all – it's always with you.

The takeaway from that is this...our positive energy is already within us. I've said it before, and I'll say it again – we make choices. Don't choose to be salty. Yes, even those of you who complain with a smile, "These computers never work – ha ha ha." Someone once told me, you can say anything you want with a smile. But here are the physics behind that; it's not so much what you say but the intension behind it. If resentment flowed through that smile, you still transmitted resentment. However, if you dig deep and hold on to a genuine desire to meet a need or solve a problem then the result will be much more favorable. A mutual bonding that you can both feel will occur. The proverbial exhale.

Allow yourself to be silly. I keep a small bottle of bubbles on my desk, a set of jacks in my purse, and I downloaded the 8 ball and the mood app on my phone just for little ways to sneak in some fun. By the way, according to my app, my mood is rambunctious.

Bottom line, just be grateful and appreciate EVERYTHING; even the stuff that feels not so fun. Walk into the world with purpose and decide to be the you, you never knew you could be. You already own it. Now claim it.

Abundance

June 1, 2011

What does abundance mean to you? Is it having lots of money? Having good health? How about an abundance of loving and supportive people in your life? Well, it's all of the above and more.

The definition of abundance is having an extremely plentiful or over sufficient quantity or supply. A person of faith believes that all their needs are met; meaning there is an abundant supply of whatever they need, be it tangible or intangible. So...if this is your reality, you're not worried right? RIGHT?

As human beings, it is very easy to fall into the habit of worry and fear. When the news is yelling out "Judgment Day" and tornadoes are taking out cities, we can't help but get in our head about things. That is your opportunity to practice faith.

It is a life certainty that something at some time will go south more than once in your lifetime. By knowing in your heart of hearts and soul of souls that everything is already alright, you can have the OM approach to those inevitable challenges. Don't beat yourself up in those moments when you feel defeated instead...ask for help, wait, and listen for those messages and messengers that will carry you through.

Remember…you choose everyday whether or not to live in your abundance. Don't let ego, judgment, or the need to fit in, cloud what you already know to be true.

Say it with me like you mean it!

- ALL my needs are met!
- ALL THINGS work for my greater good!

YES!

July 4, 2011

The long-awaited and last installment to our H.A.P.P.Y. is YES! Yes, is possibly the most wonderful word in the English language. Our YES carries with it a power that cannot be matched.

By saying YES, it's the same as saying, I'm Here! I Exist! I came to WIN!

When we say YES to life, we agree to live it; no matter what comes. Even greater than that, when we do face our challenges and ask ourselves, do I choose to live; that YES will give you the strength to go on.

Saying YES says no to negativity, no to unnecessary nonsense, no to being a bystander in your own life.

Affirmation: Say it with me...YES! I am an active participant in my life. YES!

Are the Blues Dancin' on your Happy?

September 5, 2011

No matter how happy we are at our core, the blues have a way of sneaking in. One day you're wondering..." what's wrong?" Nothing really, just a little case of the blues.

Maybe you've been so focused and so much has gotten done and now that you have a chance to slow down and rest, you're a little blue. It's really your body and spirit's way of resting. So, is it really the blues? Naw! Just a little break.

Let your body rest and relax. Just because you don't feel motivated to keep moving doesn't mean that you've given up; it means that your mind, body, and spirit need a disco nap. Take it! Get recharged and refocused and then crank it in gear again.

Fiddle Dee Dee – don't think about that today…. think about that tomorrow.

Remember – You Are Awesome and Amazing! ALWAYS!

Are you living a WORK week or a LIFE week?

February 26, 2012

I was sitting and talking with my brother about Bethany Ever After (he's such a trooper to let me watch that without complaining). The characters were talking about how many times a week they should have sex. Of course, Bethany's number was lower than Jason's. I made a comment, something to the effect of, three times a week because I'm tired from work all week, four times for a special occasion, and five times on vacation. He laughed of course and said, there's no such thing as a work week, every week is a life week. Things don't stop just because of work or whatever.

This got me thinking...I am living a work week. I treat Monday through Friday like work is all I do, and I try to squeeze everything I like and that brings me joy into two days, which is impossible. I realized, I'm living a work week and not a life week. That was powerful for me because I have been so frustrated. I finally got an idea for my next book and some other plans but man, I am just beat at the end of a day.

Every day is just that, a day! How you fill it is up to you. Yes, work is necessary but the chores, the fun, the visiting with friends, etc., shouldn't be limited just because we may have a demanding job or a job that sucks all the life out of us that we have nothing left for anything else. Sounds like a shift in thinking is in order. I too am guilty. Here are a couple of nuggets to start the shift:
First, I'm going to schedule my day and stick to

it. I was already successful in attending a Toastmasters meeting yesterday morning. Next, I'm going to think of my job as my client, not my employer. I need to get back into my entrepreneur brain. I'm thinking too much like an employee. That is death to an entrepreneur. Lastly, I'm going to go back to NO TV until 8pm. I am a TVaholic and just have it on, but it too is an energy sucker and I get little to nothing done. You too?

You all haven't heard from me in a while because my new job (which is now almost a year old) is an energy sucker. The people are so negative, the leadership is clueless of the reality of the needs of the group, and I am overwhelmed by the reality of what I said yes to. However, ... I did say yes. And I meant it. I love what I do, I just don't love the BS that come with it. That's relationships though, right? I realize that my gifts are needed there and my lesson in all this is to have the compassion and patience to recognize that they are not ready yet; but they will get there. So, what does that mean for me today?

Today, I am tasked with the challenge of putting all of this in perspective. I have my own ambitions both at work and in my life but the overall is both the same; to help people get to their happy. I love being a trainer/speaker and I'm great at it. That's right, I'm tooting my own horn, I'm great damn it!

Starting today, I challenge you to shift your thinking with me. A day is just a day. Fill it with what you want. Don't think about how tired you are, just think about your motivation, the laughter of your kids, the book you want to write, the place you want to visit, and focus on that. Even the nonsensical BS can be motivation. It certainly is mine. Let that cancel out the other stuff, the naysayers and the energy suckers. Those of you who know me, know I have a saying, "they ain't worth the spit it takes to curse 'em!" Say that to yourself whenever you feel overwhelmed by the nonsensical ridiculousness that each day can bring.

I am going to do this as well. I'd love to hear how it's going. I'm going to make an effort to tweet and Facebook when I have an "ain't worth the spit it takes to cuss 'em" moment. I'd like you to too.

Here's to having a LIFE week and doing all the things your heart desires. Keep me posted.

There's a Reason Pampers are So Thick

April 1, 2012

Why is it that when children mess up, it's called learning but when adults mess up, it's called failing? We are learning until we die.

When babies are learning to walk, they teeter onto their shaky legs, try to find their balance, and attempt that first step. They may make one or two steps, and then they lose their balance and fall. Have you noticed that when they fall, they stick their behind out a bit and then fall on their little bum? They actually have the insight to know HOW to fall. There's a reason Pampers are so thick.

So, what about us? If we were intuitive enough to know how to fall, it probably wouldn't hurt as much when the inevitable happens.

Have you ever thought about not only planning what you will do to achieve your goal but what you will do if you fall short of it, AKA, plan B. When there is a plan B, C, D, and so on, there is no need to feel the setback, just move forward with the next plan. You didn't fail, you progressed to the next level. Without whatever you did to get there, you would not have the knowledge to not only move forward but to also, not find yourself there again. I'm not saying to plan to mess up but make more rounded plans. See the whole picture because just like death is a part of life, so is learning.

Think about how you learned the things you know. When you were a teenager and watched your parents drive and thought, I can do that. But then you got behind the wheel and felt the true power of a car and said whoa!

Think about the things you learned but don't use anymore. I had a temp assignment at a deaf school. When I started, I only knew the alphabet and the happy birthday song. By the time I left, I was up to roughly 300 words and phrases. Unfortunately, not using it, has me right back to where I started. However, just like in the movie Limitless, if we tapped into some of that knowledge, I'm sure we would amaze even ourselves at what we already know.

So, I challenge you to practice, letting someone else have the last word. Practice allowing yourself to be uncomfortable. Remember, we don't learn in our successes, we learn in our missteps and in our willingness to be wrong. Step out knowing that you cannot fail. Let that give you the courage to learn and grow and move to the next level of your journey.

Sometimes to Grow Up, You Gotta Meltdown!

July 3, 2012

I speak often to my readers to be honest about how they are really feeling. I would like to share that I, your "Happy Chick," have had a meltdown. I was not paying attention to the fact that my life changed some time ago and oops, I lost track and surprise…. hello anxiety panic attack! As you can see, I still have my sense of humor so Happy Chick is still in the house! Hold on to your hats because this is going to be quite a rant; I'm about due. However, there are lessons to be learned here.

So how did this happen? Well, first was the constant relocation and ultimate landing in a very loud apartment complex in the hood. While necessary to get back on my feet, still completely out of my element. I thought I would adapt but sadly, one year later, I am still a fish out of water. I learned the lesson of humility and being grateful for what I have yet, I am still uncomfortable…for different reasons. My finances have improved so that was helpful but there is still so much to do. My relationship with my brother is incredible which is something we never shared as kids. I now have such a great support system in my family that I feel loved all the time.

Next came the job that I asked for. If I had to go back into corporate, it had to be as a trainer and it is. I work for a very noisy, very unorganized, very poorly managed, call center that has the trainer under the customer service hierarchy instead of HR where it belongs. I am surrounded by noise and sheer idiocy as it relates to training or as they call them "training opportunities." The lesson I feel I still need to learn here is compassion. I have faced my issue with authority, and I have learned to diplomatically disagree and suggest change as well as work with people whose agenda is counter intuitive to mine and still squeak out success. That is a victory! Yet, the chaos continues. God grant me compassion...and a six-figure speaking gig!

Next came Toastmasters. This is my joy. I love speaking. I love working with others to grow as a speaker and a leader. I jumped right in, and I have achieved what few have. I am the founding president of a new charter and consecutively, a Vice President of Education (the second in command) of a second club. I hold the two highest offices in two separate clubs. What a responsibility but one I am excited about. I want to fast track my way to not only DTM in the Toastmaster organization but help others grow as speakers while I too grow and move closer to the next level as a speaker and leader and earn paid gigs. I am excited about this part of my journey. Right now, I'm holding on to this piece because although there are minor frustrations – namely some people who will challenge my authority, for their own reasons, overall, I am excitedly encouraged and will face them with maturity that they don't possess yet.

Lastly, I have a new relationship. While I have chosen a person that is incredibly confident in the world, or so he seemed, behind closed doors, he is a lot of work. He is needy and clingy, and I find myself feeling like I have to choose between him and myself. Mainly because when I actively and separately work on my pursuits, he takes the position that I am deliberately trying to get away from him. Friends say that even if I love him, he still may not be suited for me. I am searching and praying for the lesson in it. We aren't children, so I would like to take the mature approach and in the words of my Sex and the City gal pals, not "jump to the dump". Yet, I know we both got excited about the prospect of marriage and children at this stage in our lives which perhaps clouded our judgment. I deeply care about this person, but I love myself more. I will continue to seek answers in the silence. I know I will be guided through the lesson, and I will be given the words to move to the next phase of my journey with him, no matter what that is.

All that and a few health concerns. WOW! So how am I still standing you might ask? Yep, that's my question too. Actually, I'm still standing because I am happy at my core. I love me and that's what matters. I know that all of this is temporary and will pass just as sure as it came. Some things will linger, and some things will fall away as I grow to my next level. Because you know…that's what really IS going on here! I am deep in the midst of transformation and growth. Growth is always happening but at our most uncomfortable, we are on the verge of the next level.

This time, I'm asking for your help. I'm going to follow my own advice and go through my book, 28 Days to Happy, beginning tomorrow – Independence Day! How's that for timing. Go through it with me, send me encouragement, strike up conversations or just follow along.

I will realign my lifestyle to fit the life I have now, and I encourage you to do the same. Here's to regaining our Happy!

Dream Big!

February 16, 2013

Remember when we were kids and someone asked, "What do you want to be when you grow up?" Back then, the sky was the limit. We wanted to be policemen, astronauts, or firemen. Some kids simply said, "I'm going to be rich or I'm going to be famous!"

I wanted to be Debbie Allen. I wanted to be Debbie Allen so bad. She was incredible. And still is for that matter. In 1994, the year of the Lion King, she was choreographing the Oscars and I went to audition. I had prepared a song I sang often from the movie Fame, Out Here on My Own. But, when I got there and saw Debbie Allen, live and in person, my nerves took over and I stopped being an entertainment professional and was just a fan. I tried to gather my nerves and then I started hearing all the wonderful talent that was there, and on top of the nerves, I began to doubt myself. I just wanted to go home. Then I thought…. HOME, that's a song. That's a song I do well, ok, I'll do home. Then it was my turn, my idol, a woman I thought was the epitome of the most talented person on the planet, called my name, little o'l me. Debbie Allen called out Leslie Pogue. My breath left my body. I pulled it together enough to stand in front of her and tell her I will be singing Home, from The Wiz. She said to begin when I was ready, and I began to sing.

Unfortunately, I only sang the first verse. How could I do that? Everybody knows the best part is at the end. When I got to my car, I proceeded to bang the crap out of my steering wheel because I was so disgusted with myself. I couldn't believe that I blew what felt like the only moment in time for me to become a super star. I realized I lost sight of the objective. I was so overwhelmed by Debbie Allen that I was a fan when I should have been a professional.

Many years later, in a totally different capacity I decided to change careers. I was sick of being an executive assistant and took a personality quiz to see what I would be best suited for. Everything led me to training and speaking. With my entertainment background it seemed perfect.

I'd been to some SkillPath Seminars, and I really liked their trainers, so I decided that I wanted to be a SkillPath Trainer. I submitted an application and soon they were holding auditions in Los Angeles. I was sent the subject matter to create a mini class. The subject was the Indispensable Assistant. I created the best training. I worked hard on my PowerPoint presentation, my timing, and how not to stand in front of the overhead. Then the time came. Of course, there had to be a wow factor, so I played copy written material. And even though I told them it was just for this audition; it was more of a crime that I treated that audition as a rehearsal instead of an actual class. All I showed them is that I knowingly defied the rules. Once again, I lost site of the goal. I was crushed and sad for a bit, but I said I'm going to work for SkillPath! My destiny was with SkillPath!

So, I re-applied and I got another shot except this time, if I wanted it, I had to go get it. I had to find the money to get to Kansas. I used some vacation days and spent some of my rent for a plane ticket. This time, I was more than ready. I had my subject matter, I had my PowerPoint, and I had my wow factor. I shook their hands; I was called into the tiny room, and I was a trainer! I made great eye contact; I loaded my presentation and commenced with a mock class. I was in the moment and doing it for the love of training! At the end of my presentation, I closed with this quote; the journey of a thousand miles, begins with a single step. I took a step that day toward my big dream and I finally got the gig!

My mom didn't get her degree until she was 51 years old. Winston Churchill did not become prime minister of England until he was 62 years old, Henry Ford failed and went broke 5 times before he finally succeeded, and Pepsi Cola went bankrupt 3 times.

Dare to dream. Never let anyone tell you that you cannot do exactly what you want to do. There will almost always be a line that can circle a city block of people that will tell you how you CAN'T do something. Never be at the front of that line.

So today I ask you to listen to that kid inside and tell the grown up to just hush and Dream Big!

If Life Were Santa's Lap, I'd Be the One Crying

April 29, 2013

Today I noticed a picture on a co-worker's desk. It was a picture of her kids sitting on Santa's lap. In the picture, her son was crying.

It made me think about all the pictures I've seen of kids on Santa's lap, including my own with my little brother, and usually it is the boy that's crying.

When I shared that with my co-worker, she asked what about now? My brother is one of the steadiest people I know and me on the other hand…well, you've read my blogs. I heard myself say to her that if life were Santa's lap, I'd be the one crying. How many of you feel that way too?

It's not that things are so bad but whenever you go through a transition, it can be difficult. I am building a business and branching out as a speaker and along with maintaining the regular life stuff, some days I just want to throw a fit on the floor.

What I do when I feel that way is I do exactly what I've written about in my blogs. I take baby steps toward my tasks, and I spend vegetative time just doing nothing. When I honor whatever, I'm feeling at that moment and allow it to move through me, it does exactly that, it moves through me and I'm able to get on with the things that matter.

It is fine to want to throw a fit and go kicking and screaming. Life can be pretty random. For all the planning we do, there are things we simply cannot foresee. In those moments, have your quiet, behind closed doors tantrum. Then, dust yourself off, stand straight in line and just smile for the camera. Cheese!

Confront Your Fate

April 22, 2013

It is said that we all have a fate, a destiny. Do you know your fate? What is it you are supposed to be doing?

Getting off your journey is a little like playing hooky. You know where you are supposed to be, but you have made a choice to be somewhere else or do something else.

The choices we make every day are like that. When you feel that uneasy feeling in the pit of your stomach or you get that inkling that something isn't right, you are choosing to go off track. This pulls you further away from your fate. But when you are following your path, it's smooth and natural. Everything seems to fit and come easy. This is a sign you are moving toward your fate.

So how do you know what your fate is? Your fate is a series of steppingstones. Each step moves you closer to your joy. When you are living in your joy, the choices and actions that led there are purposeful and intended.

Have you ever looked at your life and said, "how did I get here?" That is a clear sign you have moved away from your fate. But you can't escape your fate. Life has a way of always putting us back on track.

Think about your life. I know for me, I have come, not quite full circle but I see the pattern. I now know where I zigged off course and now, I can feel that I'm back on the right road.

If you can't see where you went off course, you are possibly still off course. The indicator of that is if things seem a little bumpy or constantly challenging. It may be time to examine and retrace your steps to see how to get back on the path that feeds your soul. It's not going to happen in one big leap but once you've identified that you are off track, you can plot a course to get back on track and move toward your fate.

Enjoy the journey – don't worry about the destination.

Back to the Middle

April 15, 2013

One of my favorite songs by Indie Arie is Back to the Middle. What speaks to me the loudest is the bridge where she says, "You gotta take the good with the bad, and you might hit the wall. Sometimes you'll fly and sometimes you will fall. There ain't any way, to avoid the pain but it's getting burned, that's how you will learn to come back to the middle.

Many of my speeches and posts speak about how we learn in our mistakes or when we fall. It is so important to just get back up. That too is often the hardest.

During my walk today, I was thinking about the difference between struggling with a job and struggling without one. Oddly, struggling without one is so much more pleasant. No one likes or wants to struggle but if that is your journey at the moment, wouldn't it be so much better if you could also go sit by the ocean and think in the middle of a Tuesday? Wouldn't it be great if you could accept an invitation to go play a round of golf or go do some writing in the library? Take a moment and think about all the people you know with a job. Do they like it? Are they just staying there because of the presumed security in an unstable economy? Here's a thought…When is our economy ever not unstable?

Now think about the people you know who have lost their job. How are they facing every day? I'm sure some are having a rough time both financially and emotionally. Some have gotten past that part and entered acceptance and have either decided to do something on their own or they just do what they can when they can. Of the two groups of people who you know, which group seems to be the most at peace?

I'm in no way suggesting that anyone give up their job but what I am suggesting is that you look at your life in a more rounded way. When you have a steady income, that is the best time to start trying out some of your dreams. It is usually an issue of energy. An unhappy employee rarely has any energy left to indulge in their own dreams. They just want to go to sleep and put an end to that day. Find the energy to end the day on something that is about you. Even if you only spend a little time on it. A single drop of rain can create a pond.

I will end with this thought, also from Indie Arie, "Don't make no mind about falling down, 'cause it's when you're in that valley you can see both sides more clearly. Come back to the middle."

A Spring Song

April 8, 2013

Spring is supposed to bring new life but spring for me has always only meant all the bugs are out again. Now, don't misunderstand, I like spring, I just don't like those darn bugs.

Isn't life the same way? There are things we look forward to in our life; a new job, a new love, traveling, and staying out late but for all the greatness, there are still things we don't like. Spring also means taxes, spring cleaning, and allergies. But isn't it funny how we don't let that stop us from having our fun?

In the words of Maya Angelou, a bird doesn't sing because it has an answer, it sings because it has a song. What is your song this spring?

I've said it many times before that it is always best to begin at the beginning so, before you start, think about what you want to do. Is it a fun project like a new hobby or revisiting an old one? I am inspired to take up making oil candles again. I really enjoyed it and people liked getting them as gifts. Photography was another hobby I enjoyed that I am considering revisiting.

Or are you considering a new business venture Maybe turning that hobby into a thriving business. Try not to lose your creativity in the business of it. Have fun whatever your endeavor.

How about those who feel uninspired to do anything. You all are the most special of all because you have the gift of all the vast universe. Your challenge is to choose. Spring is a time of resurrection and sometimes what we need most is to resurrect our own spirit. Take small steps. Go to places that motivate you like maybe the ocean, sit in a cafe and people watch, walk barefoot in the park, or even in your own grassy yard. The key is to remember that it is not about what you produce, it's about how you feel. Once your spirit in at peace, all things will become clear and then you will produce results; but don't rush it. Just be for a while.

Find 5-10 minutes of quiet time just for you (even if you have to sneak it in while in the bathroom). Do yourself inventory and gauge how you feel from deep inside. Acknowledge what you are thankful for and ask for help to grow more into your best you.

Remember to sing and embrace ALL the aspects of spring because even butterflies are bugs.

Be Legendary

May 13, 2013

When I think of the word legendary, I think of.... well, actually, I think of Barney Stinson for you How I Met Your Mother fans.

But then after that, I think of people like Maya Angelou, Jimmy Hendrix, Bob Marley, Celia Cruz, Hemingway, Shakespeare, and one of my favorites, Henry VIII. He was just so wakadoodle. These are just a few of many legendary people who come to mind. However, there are legendary people all around us. The survivors of 9/11 are legendary. The three women who survived a 10-year kidnapping or any person that ultimately survives being held in captivity is legendary. Cancer survivors that we know and don't know are legendary. The 104-year-old aunt that can still fry her own chicken and remembers all the names of her nieces and nephews is legendary.

So, what does all that mean? Well, I mention these things because we tend to over think when we hear words like legendary. It is so massive that it can shut us down in our tracks. I was watching Michael Beckwith and he said that when we think of abundance and prosperity we automatically think of money, when we think of love we automatically think of a person, and when we think of infinite intelligence we think of intellect, but that is not what it means. We have to not just think bigger in general but think of ourselves bigger.

I have literally seen greatness happen before me. Not that it was so grandiose but simple things. I was working this week and I wanted donuts on a non donut day and magically, there were donuts in the kitchen. I went parking at the beach and wanted an unobstructed view of the water and the spot I was going to pull in was overrun by a man and his dogs, so I drove a little further up and there it was, an unobstructed view of the water. The best one, and I think I shared this one, but it bears repeating, I had been putting off getting a money order for my rent and even on the day I finally said I was going to do it, something told me not to so I delayed and when I got home my landlord told me I owe less than usual because I overpaid. I don't even know how I could even do that but WOW! What a gift. That is legendary stuff.

Facing your life and doing your best every day is the stuff of legends. Everyone doesn't get the opportunity to greet each day and make a difference in it. You have been gifted a new day. To be legendary just means to be present. If you show up, you will be seen, greeted, observed, noticed, and to someone you will be the example that changes their life.

So how legendary will you be today?

Going Deep

May 6, 2013

I was talking with a friend of mine today and we were talking about writing. More specifically, telling our story. You know, the personal aspects of our lives. Celebrities have done it. Politicians have done it. Artists have done it. They all have GONE DEEP!

What does that mean???? Going deep means going to that place within, that most of us run from. When you hear spoken word that touches you to your core, that poet probably went deep to share their inner most self.

Sharing aspects of your deepest self leaves you raw! Exposed! Naked!

When you decide to go deep, it will be the start of a level of healing that can't be measured. Once you go deep – you are free.

But BEWARE! When you decide to go on that journey, bake in some exits. You will need some self-care mechanisms like comfort food, time with friends, and isolation time. Also, know, there is no turning back. Once you open Pandora's box, it's open. The risk is high, but the reward is great!

I will share that I have not yet gone deep, but I am preparing for the journey. I may even have a title for my book (Happy Chick – One Chicks Way of Dealing with Life) Sound Familiar? Everything I have ever done has led me to this point. I can feel my spirit freeing as I continue to grow. Memories are resurfacing, emotions are zigzagging, and I am seeing things so clearly that my needs are landing in my lap before I need them. It is almost time for me to go deep. Like my many posts before, when I do, I will take you with me, but I am strong enough to admit that I'm not ready yet.

Soon!

Control or Service?

June 24, 2013

Some people are deemed "control" freaks. I got to thinking about that. I was watching an old episode of Grey's Anatomy and there was a patient that had OCD and Cristina, a very strong, very "A" personality person was tending to him. He said that they were alike. The difference is that she had found a constructive way to channel her energy as a surgeon and his energy took the form of OCD which is just another "A" personality type of control. Hmmmmm???

If you have someone in your life who always wants to drive, who wants to be the host, who is always making themselves available for the family and friend events that arise at the last-minute, perhaps they just want to be of service. Yes, they may have some control issues too but, think of the whole person. Are they also philanthropists? Are they volunteers? Do they find pleasure in the planning and organizing of things…anything?? So cut 'em a break! Cut yourself a break – if you are this person.

I am that person. Yes, I like control, for various reasons. However, I also, enjoy having people to take care of. I enjoy having a hand in serving a group of people and educating them about themselves. I love the ah ha moment! Is that control? NO! I love to serve. Most people think I am selfish and self-absorbed. I'm a single woman with no kids, of course I'm selfish and self-absorbed. Who else do I have to think about? That is why I am of service. In service, I get to help. I get to be a mother, a nurse, a counselor, a friend, another set of hands, a neutral party, an unbiased sounding board, and so much more. I also get to grow myself because I have put myself in a position of follower and as I've said before, the best leaders, know how to follow. There are so many opportunities to practice.

Stop and think before you judge. Not every control freak needs to be in control all the time. Sometimes they just want to be of service.

So let them.

The Silent Champion

June 10, 2013

Silence is Golden. That is never truer than when we are listening. How does that serve you? By listening, you are privy to needs, fears, plans, and the desires of those around you. That is valuable information for negotiation and service.

Many people have commented that I don't say much but when I do speak, I say things that are insightful and profound. While I appreciate the compliment, I just listen. I have learned not to speak until asked or until I have something of value to add.

It is helpful as we move through our journey and rise, that we learn to be stealth. What I mean by that is to do your homework. Read, be current and relevant, know your audience (that includes family), and most important of all...never show your hand.

When you speak, speak with purpose. As you get more comfortable with this, your self-confidence will skyrocket! You will know that you know, and you will see it rollover into your professional life as well.

Listen! Speak with Purpose! Watch the Rewards!

Acceptance

July 8, 2013

In our current political climate, acceptance seems to be what is needed. The latest rulings on prop 8 in California and the voting ruling each send very distinct messages for where we are as a nation.

Regardless of your view on either subject we all have to accept the rulings passed. A select group of voices were heard, considered, and an action was taken.

How often do you find yourself fighting against the ruling? A company rule or policy, the continual negative behavior of another person, or your own circumstance. Sometimes until the next action is discovered, acceptance is what is required.

Acceptance doesn't mean settling, which I am firmly against. Acceptance is merely taking inventory of your situation from all angles and understanding fully what you are working with; what tools you have and who your allies are. The peace that comes from acceptance allows for a solution or guidance to come your way.

You're not Scarlet O'Hara – You Just a Little Black Girl

October 16, 2017

My second favorite movie of all time is Gone with the Wind and I often joke that I'm like

Scarlet O'Hara. I often say, "I won't think about that now, I'll think about that tomorrow!" I never like to be uncomfortable, I always like to be the center of attention, and I'm used to getting my way and what I want. But like Scarlet, that can come with some ridicule.

However, if anyone that has seen Gone with the Wind paid attention, they saw that Scarlet was an amazingly strong woman. She always did what was necessary when it really counted. She took care of her family after the War and even after she was rich. She was true to her word, she was a savvy businesswoman, she always went after what she wanted even if she was in a little bit of danger, and she wasn't afraid to stand up for herself; in the words of Ret Butler, "what a woman!"

But, because she is white and slaves are involved, most people of color look at me with the side eye when I make that comparison; most of which haven't and won't even see the movie.

Scarlet exemplifies a strong and brave woman, no matter what color. She survived war, starvation, displacement, personal attack, widowhood, poverty, ridicule, loss of a child, and what turned out to be the love of her life. She was a daughter, a sister, a wife, and a mother. She had a deep faith in God and love of the land, aka Tara. She was there for her friends and family and was never afraid to just be herself. That is why I identify with Scarlet O'Hara, plus the southern thang. I'm half city and half southern. I gotta say, I embrace my southern most of all. But I digress....

When some people see others who are comfortable in their skin, they may try to project their own insecurities onto them. The name calling, the cutting digs, and the passive aggressive conversations are all a neon sign that you are dealing with someone that is not at your level. Depending on what you need to do, you may have to continue to deal with that person. If you don't, they will fall away organically. However, like the first "P" in your HAPPY, give yourself permission to stay true to you and meet them where they are. In other words, you don't need to cut them back, just extract what you need from the interaction and move on.

Most of all remember this – at the end of the day, it's not what they call you, it's what you answer to.

Now Go! Be! Do!

I Am!

July 1, 2013

I am happy
I am living an abundant life
I am gracefully moving through my journey
I am authentic when I show up in the world
I am a whole person
I am worthy of love
I am an amazing being
I am the victor of my life
I am hot!
I am brilliant
I am awake and enlightened
I am of service to those who need me
I am scrappy
I am courageous
I am human with human emotions
I am open to the possibilities

I am safe, protected, and loved in all that I do
I am becoming the person I want in my life
I am able to meet people where they are
I am kind – I am smart – I am important
I am able to laugh at myself
I am passionate
I am still learning and growing
I am secure in myself enough to admit when I'm wrong
I am able to ask for help
I am able to say no!
I am more likely to ask for forgiveness than permission
I am independent

Always remember who you are!

PERMISSION TO REPRINT

Permission to reprint articles by Leslie Pogue, is hereby given to all print, broadcast, and electronic media provided that the contact information at the end of each article is included in your publication. Organizations publishing articles electronically, a live, click-able link to https://www.lpspeak.com must also be included with the body of the article. Additionally, please mail one copy of your publication to:

LP Speak, 13428 Maxella Avenue #556, Marina del Rey, CA 90292

    1. Permission to reprint articles by Leslie Pogue, at no charge is granted with the agreement that:

        a. The article bio be included following each article used.

        b. One copy of the publication in which the article is published be provided to LP Speak.

c. A fee per article will be expected for articles published without the closing bio and contact information; $300.

2. Permission is also granted for reasonable: Editing content and industry specific example exchange.
   - Length.
   - Article title change.

3. Electronic publishing of articles must include a live, click-able link to **https://www.lpspeak.com**.

Any questions, please send email to **Leslie@lpspeak.com**.

Go! Be! Do!

The Positive Side of Bad Stuff
is a collection of blogs I've written over the last several years. It speaks primarily to the personal behaviors that we all manage every day from joy to grief; from who cares to self-care.

It will give you a guide to make sense of the issues in your life and find your own Positive Side of the Bad Stuff. Big Hug!

www.ingramcontent.com/pod-product-compliance
Lightning Source LLC
Chambersburg PA
CBHW061732040426
42453CB00027B/2175